1   Hint Fuerteventura... in a different way!

By Andrea Müller

Comments and questions are welcome:
Andrea Müller
Calle Las Cuevas, 91 - A2
E- 35542 Punta Mujeres, province of Las Palmas, Lanzarote
Web: www.lanzarote-mal-anders.de
mailto:ebook@lanzarote-mal-anders.de

© 2019 by Andrea Müller, cover design: Andrea Müller
Number of pages Printing variant: 61 pages
Number of images: 1 image

2 Imprint (German)

Bibliographic Information of the German National Library

The German National Library lists this publication in the German National Bibliography; detailed bibliographic data are available on the Internet at http://dnb.d-nb.de

Production and publishing
BoD - Books on Deman, Norderstedt

ISBN: 9783749448487

3   Overview map Fuerteventura

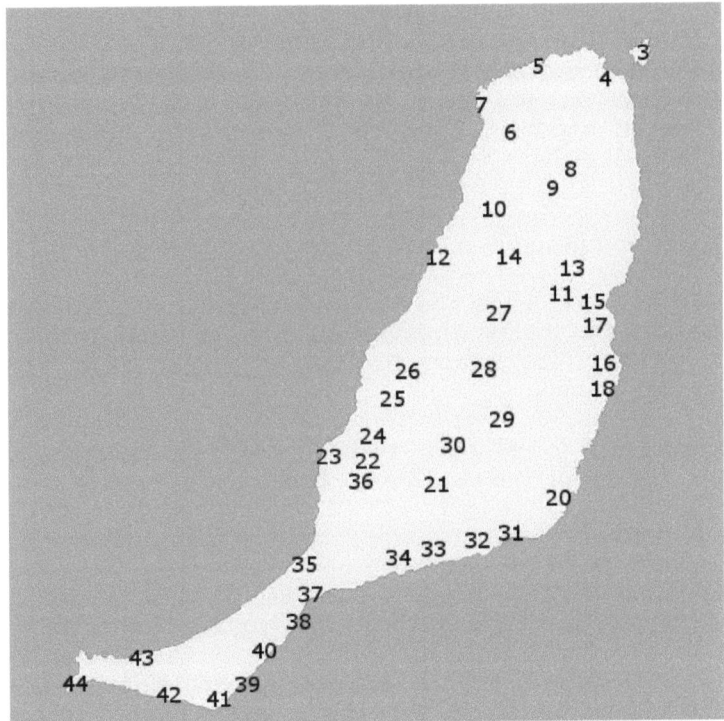

3=Los Lobos, **4**= Corralejo, **5**= Playa de Majanicho/
Popcornstrand, **6**= Lajares, **7**= El Cotillo, **8**= Villaverde,
9= La Oliva, **10**= Tindaya, **11**= Casas de Filipito, **12**=
Puertito de los Molinos, **13**= Tetir, **14**= Tefia, **15**= Puerto del
Rosario, **16**= Caleta de Fueste, **17**= Playa la Guirra, **18**=
Salinas del Carmen, **20**= Pozo Negro, **21**= Tuineje, **22**=
Pajara, **23**= Ajui, **24**= Vego de Rio Palmas, **25**= Betancuria,
26= Mirador de Morro Velosa, **27**= La Ampuyenta, **28**=
Antigua, **29**= Valles de Ortega, **30**= Tiscamanita, **31**= Las
Playitas, **32**= Gran Tarajal, **33**= Tarajalejo, **34**= La Lajita,
35= La Pared,
36= Mirador Astronomico de Sicasumbre, **37**= Costa Calma,
38= Playas de Sotavento, **39**= Playas de Jandia, **40**= Risco
del Paso, **41**= Jandia, **42**= Morro Jable,
43= Cofete, **44**= Puerto de la Cruz

4 Fuerteventura - An overview

Second edition 2019 - Up-to-date, detailed information, important useful insider tips and all highlights.

The **Fuerteventura travel guide... a different kind of guide!** takes you next to endlessly long, snow-white Caribbean beaches to the attractions of the multifaceted volcanic island.

In the north, from the largest and liveliest town **Corralejo,** explore the beautiful dunes, the small nature protected **Isla Los Lobos**, where the former lighthouse keeper runs a small restaurant, and enjoy the beautiful **beaches** of the **Playas Grandes**, which are especially suitable for water sports in the sections **Flag Beach**, Playa **Bajo Negro, Playa Moro** and **Playa Poris.**

In the northwest, visit the fishing village of **El Cotillo, which** protects the coast from intruders with its centuries-old defensive tower, the **Castillo de Testón.**

Look from the coast to the long beaches of **Playa del Castillo**, where kite- and bodysurfers meet.

Make a detour to the **lighthouse Faro de Tostón** with the **fishing museum** and don't miss the yet unknown **popcorn beach**.

Visit the historic town of **La Oliva**, whose monuments include the parish church of **Nuestra Señora de la Candelaria**, the **Ermita de Puerto Rico**, the impressive **Casa del Coroneles**, the dilapidated **Casa del Inglés** and the former **La Cilla** granary, dating back to the 17th century. Art lovers can admire the works of well over 80 artists in the spacious **Casa Mané.**

In Tindaya, in the **Casa Alta de Tindaya,** marvel at the unique rock carvings of the Guanches, the native inhabitants of the Canary Islands.

Discover the **monument to the poet Unamuno** and taste the goat's cheese at the **Quesos de Tindaya** cheese dairy.

Immerse yourself in the traditional rural life of the island at the **Ecomuseo de La Alcogida** open-air museum in **Tefía** and acquire genuine local handicrafts.

In the little-visited village of **Tetír,** next to the listed **parish church of Santo Domingo de Guzman**, you will find the **Gofio Museum**, run by the last active Gofio miller in the world.

In the island capital **Puerto del Rosario,** Fuerteventura's largest shopping centre, **Las Rotondas,** awaits you by offering extensive shopping in specialist shops.
Explore the centre with the **Nuestra Señora del Rosario** parish church, the **Casa Museo Unamuno museum,** buy fresh local produce in the **Mercado Municipal** or the **Mercado Agrario de Fuerteventura.**

Treat yourself to a sunbath at the city beach **Playa Chica** or at the main beach **Playa Blanca.**
In the large popular holiday resort **Caleta de Fustes** you can enjoy the view of the marina from the gently sloping sandy beach, **Playa de Castillo.**
Along the long promenade, past historic **lime kilns,** you reach the shopping centre **Centro Comercial Atlantico.**

In addition, the popular **African market** offers further shopping opportunities.
Explore the **Salinas del Carmen,** the historic saltworks with the **Museo de La Sal,** where salt was still extracted in the 1980s for the fish factory in Puerto del Rosario.
In the centre of Fuerteventura you will meet even more **island history:** During a guided tour through **La Ampuyenta** you will see the small but impressive **Ermita de San Pedro de Alcántara** and learn all the details in the house, the **Casa Museo Dr. Mena** and the **hermitage of Fray Andresito.**
In sleepy **Antigua,** go to the windmill, the **Molino de Antigua,** with its interesting cheese museum, the **Museo de Queso de Majoro.**

You should definitely stop in **Tuineje** to see the altarpieces of the **battle of Tamasite** in the church of **San Miguel Arcángel,** which show the battle won by the islanders against the English.
In Pájara, visit the impressive **Nuestra Señora de la Regla** parish church, in front of which there is a **Noria,** a restored waterwheel driven by a donkey.

Drive to the rugged coast of **Ajuy** with the deep black beach of the dead, **Playa de los Muertos,** and explore the **lime kilns** along the sea cliffs, as well as the deep caves, the Cuevas, which served as pirate hiding places.

In the former island capital **Betancuria** you should visit the church **Nuestra Señora de la Concepción** with the attached museum of **sacral art** and the monastery ruins of the **Convento de San Buenaventura** with the **Ermita San Diego.**

Look from the 645 m high vantage point, the **Mirador de Morro Velosa,** onto the desert-like landscape of the island. You must make Selfies at the **Mirador de Guise y Ayose,** the 4.50 m high statues of the former kings who ruled over the island.

If you want to see how old **windmills** work on the island, you can do so in the small museum, the **Centro de Interpretación de Molinos** in **Tiscamanita**. During a detour to the **Quesos de Belido** cheese dairy, you will even come across filled gofio biscuits.
Cross the impassable **Malpais** of the aborigines, interspersed with boulders and lava stones, and turn back time in the stone-built settlement of **La Atalayita.**
If you meet on the east coast the large holiday settlement **Las Playitas**, with a dark, fine sandy beach, you must in any case approach the unique lighthouse, the **Faro Punta de la Entallada.**

In **Gran Tarajal**, on the fine sandy dark beach, you will meet locals who live here and work in hotels.
In **Tarajalejo** you meet an almost German enclave with an R2 hotel and apartments, which leads along a long promenade with a dark pebble beach. Worth mentioning are the new 5 sculptures of the **Mareseum**, which represent the interpretation "the sea and all that it constitutes and conveys".
You should definitely spend a nice day in **La Lajita** in the huge **Oasis Park**, where children will also get their money's worth thanks to the impressive shows.
Let yourself be impressed by the unique contrast of a barren mountain landscape and a miniature Sahara: Experience in **La Pared** at the narrowest point of the island, the **Istmo de la Pared**, a rough coast with beautiful bays, look north at the large **rock gate,** or face the waves of the Atlantic Ocean at the **Playa de Viejo Rey.** Don't miss the **La Pastora** cheese dairy, which offers goat's milk liqueur as well as sheep's and goat's cheese.

Feel at home on the <u>Costa Calma</u>, which is preferred by German holidaymakers, but with a beautiful beach location and sun guarantee. Shop in the **shopping centres**, stroll through the **African market** or enjoy **tapas** and the typical German cuisine with a freshly tapped Pilsner.

An absolute must is the more than **20 km long beach section** that starts after the **Costa Calma**, leads over **Jandía Playa** and ends in the former fishing village <u>Morro Jable.</u>
Take a break at the snow-white beach with crystal-clear turquoise sea, and let your soul simply dangle.
From the Playa **de Sotavento** to the **Risco del Paso** you will also get your money's worth thanks to the **René Egli Wind- and Kite- Surf Center**, from beginners to professionals.
In the south of Fuerteventura you can swim in the beautiful bays of the **Playa de Butihondo** and the **Playa de Esquinzo** and continue endless relaxing beach walks to the south of the island to **Morro Jable.**
Relax at the **Playas de Jandía**, go shopping on the long shopping promenade in Jandía and enjoy the most beautiful stretch of beach, **Playa del Matorral,** which is particularly suitable for children.
From the harbour town of **Morro Jable**, head for the southern tip of Fuerteventura. Reach the sleepy village of <u>Puerto de la Cruz</u> with the lighthouse **Faro de Jandía** via jerky volcanic tracks.
Take the serpentines to <u>Cofete</u> and the endlessly long **Playa de Barlovento** with its incredible surf, and visit the historic **Villa Winter**, where the rumour kitchen is boiling.

5 La Isla de Los Lobos

The only 6 square kilometers small island, **Isla de Los Lobos,** originated with the north of Fuerteventura about 6000- 8000 years ago and lies between the neighboring island Lanzarote and Fuerteventura in the strait La Bocaina. The name of the island comes from the monk seals, the Lobos marineros, who lived before and on the island in the 15th century. Out of fear for the fishermen's dwindling fish stocks, the hunt for the seals, which had been exterminated within a century, was released.

In 1863 the lighthouse was built, which still today shows the way to the ships in the fairway La Bocaina between Lanzarote and Fuerteventura, as well as the strait El Rio, between Los Lobos and Fuerteventura.

After the lighthouse was automated in 1968, the otherwise unemployed lighthouse keeper was allowed to open a fish restaurant in the harbour to entertain the day guests.

Thanks to successful protests, neither building sins nor tourist development measures took place on Los Lobos. In 1982 the island was declared a **Natural Park**, the **Parque Natural**, and in 1987 it was integrated into the Dune National Park of Corralejo.

The ticket office is located in the port of Corralejo, a glass bottom boat for the crossing starts directly opposite.

Already after 15 minutes crossing one has arrived on the island.

The way leads over the concrete landing stage to the visitor centre, the **Centro de Visitantes**, where there are information boards and toilets.

Now you have to decide if you want to explore the island to the right or to the left. Since only officially approved hiking trails are open, follow the signs.

If one starts the walk over the island in direction to the lighthouse, the Faro de Martiño, one meets after 10 minutes the small harbour **El Puertito** with the restaurant of the former lighthouse keeper and a bath possibility in the crystal clear lagoon.

The way to the **Las Lagunitas** continues along houses that have almost fallen apart in the meantime.

Las Lagunitas is characterised by the plants that can grow in Jandía, in the region of El Saladar, in spite of the sea water, similar to those in the south of Fuerteventura.

Afterwards a bright sandy road, which passes by the boiling black coast, leads to the lighthouse.

The route continues to **Montaña Caldera**, which can be climbed in 30-40 minutes at 127 metres.

Then you can visit the saltworks, **Las Salinas del Carmen**, which have been restored but never put into operation.

Shortly after, there is one of the most beautiful beaches of the island, the **Playa de La Calera**.

Conclusion: The crossing from the port of Corralejo takes only 15 minutes. However, it takes at least 3 hours to

circumnavigate the island. In addition: To climb the Montaña de Caldera, there are at least 45 minutes for the ascent and 30 minutes for the descent.
Tip: In case of a clear view, one should start the tour over the island on the left side in order to first climb the 127 m high volcanic mountain, the Montaña de Caldera. A beautiful view over Los Lobos, Lanzarote and Fuerteventura is guaranteed.

6 Corralejo

In the 1950s, **Corralejo** was still a small fishing nest, with a few tiny dwellings and just 200 inhabitants. From 1968 onwards, it developed into a lively holiday resort in the north of the island.

When in 1982 the unique, breathtaking dune landscape south of the city was placed under strict conservation, 2 hotel bunkers, the RIU Tres Islas and the RIU Oliva Beach were already there.
Through the 20 square kilometres large area, the dead straight country road FV-1 leads to the island capital Puerto del Rosario.
On the coast, the flying sand blowing over from the Famara area of the neighbouring island of Lanzarote created dreamlike bathing bays on more than 7 kilometres of snow-white, lava-covered bays.
For further hotels only a building permit was granted outside the dunes and south of the city.
Corralejo now boasts more than 20,000 guest beds and is one of the most visited holiday destinations on the island, along with Caleta de Fueste, on the coast in the centre of the island and Jandía in the south.
In the **ferry port**, the **Puerto de Corralejo**, boats start to transfer to the offshore island Los Lobos or to the neighbouring island Lanzarote. Alternatively there is the possibility to take the big ferries from Fred Olsen or Armas to Lanzarote, so that you can also take a car with you.

On a clear day, from the promenade, the **Punta de Corralejo**, which goes along the left side of the harbour, one can enjoy a beautiful view to Lanzarote and Los Lobos.
To the right of the harbour begins the beach promenade, the **Avenida Maritima**, which leads past innumerable restaurants and cafés, as well as small beach bays.

In the centre of Corralejo, the long **Avenida Nuestra Señora del Carmen** invites you to go shopping.

At the end of the village towards the main beaches, the Playas Grandes, is the **Villa Tabaiba Galeria de Arte**. It is privately owned and only opened on an irregular basis. Nevertheless, it is worth taking a look over the wall of the property to admire the works of art.
On the main beaches, the signposted **Playas Grandes**, which lie in front of the RIU hotels, the beautiful snow-white dunes and sandy beaches present themselves in their full splendour.

The beach at the RIU hotels can also be reached by public bus or taxi, while a rental car is recommended for the following bays, **Playa Bajo Negro**, **Playa del Moro** and **Playa del Porís**, which are particularly recommended for kite and body surfers.

Markets:
6.1 *Mercado Baku*
The market is located at the Baku Water Park in Corralejo. On Tuesdays and Fridays, imitations can be purchased between 10.00 and 14.00 hours.

6.2 *Mercado El Campanario*
The large market is located in the **shopping center El Campanario** in Calle Hibisco, in Corralejo. On Thursdays and Sundays between 10.00 and 14.00 local handicrafts are offered. The centre's shops are also open.

7 Acua- Waterpark

The water park of over 25,000 sqm is located in Avenida Nuestra Señora del Carmen 41, in Corralejo. 13 water slides, a wave pool, Jacuzzis, children's zones and a restaurant are available. Sunbeds and parasols are free of charge. Opening hours and admission fees at: www.acuawaterpark.com

8 Playa de Majanicho and Popcorn Beach

There are 2 ways to reach the beaches. The picturesque Playa de Majanicho can be reached from Lajares towards the north.

With a little luck you will see local fishermen preparing their fish for lunch.
The sand road, with a view of the neighbouring island Lanzarote, leads along further beaches.
After approx. 10 further driving minutes one meets an illegal beach hut boarded together, made of in large parts with flotsam and jetsam.
Right in front of it is the popcorn beach, which lives up to its name.
Coming from Corralejo, the way to these beaches is a little harder to find. Coming from the port, on the road to the main bus station, on Avenida Juan Carlos, you will find Hotel Bristol Sunset Beach on the left. On the right there is a road sign for Puerto del Rosario, La Oliva, Cotillo, Aeropuerto, Estacion de Autobuses, Grandes Playas and **Mjanicho** (to the right).
Shortly after, a zebra crossing follows, where you turn right into an inconspicuous path, on the sides of which cars are parked in the upper part. Now follow the sandy road towards the coast.

9   Lajares

The small village, which has the charm of a hippie Eldorado, is a popular stop for surfers on their way to the coast to El Cotillo.
Lajares became famous for its artisan school, the **Escuela de Artesania Canaria**, which has a long tradition.
Background: The embroidery introduced by Portuguese immigrants was in full bloom from the end of the 19th to the beginning of the 20th century. Returners from America and Portugal employed the women of the village as cheap labourers who were underpaid due to greed for profit.

The founder of the school, Mrs. Natividad Hernandez Lopez, paid the workers fairly and founded the embroidery school in 1957 to train more women. In the meantime it is connected to one of the biggest handicraft shops of the island, in which beside arts and crafts, Aloe Vera products, clothes and food are sold.
The shop is not separately signposted, but still easy to find. At the end of the village, directly next to the pharmacy, the Farmacia, there is a lottery place which is a souvenir shop in the truest sense of the word next to gambling.

Every Saturday from 10.00 to 14.00 a small **hippie market** with handmade souvenirs takes place in the centre.

In the past, grain cultivation played a major role alongside goat farming.
In the district **Casas de Arriba** there are 2 Canarian Gofio **windmills**, in which the roasted grain was processed into flour.
The round windmill, which is still being restored, is a Molino, the female counterpart is called Molina, with a corner building for the miller. The **Ermita San Antonio** is located on the large paved square.

10 El Cotillo
The place is located in the northwest on the coast of the island, at the end of FV-10.
The former fishing village was extended by numerous new buildings and apartments.
At the entrance of the village to the sea side there is a restored **windmill**, which should be worth a photo.
In the sign-posted village towards **El Tostón**, above the new harbour, there are restored **lime kilns** that look like small fortresses and remind of the once important economic role of the village. For a long time, lime production was Fuerteventura's most important source of income and was mainly sold in Gran Canaria.
Above is the most important historical monument of the town: the **Castillo de El Tostón**.
The history of the fortified tower begins with the conquest of the island by the Spanish crown. The bastion was built in the 17th century on the ruins of the old Castillo, the Rico Roque with stones, which lies from a cave near El Castillo. The aim was to protect the coast and the harbour from the frequent attacks of the North African pirates, English and French.
The tower has a diameter of 15 m and tapers upwards. In the basement there was the powder chamber, on the roof there were 3 iron cannons and a water cistern, which enabled the 12 soldiers to remain self-sufficient for a longer period of time.
There is a temporary exhibition in the fortified tower. The entrance fee of 1.50 € can only be paid with
paid for with a credit card. Children under the age of 12 are free.

By the way: an identically constructed defensive tower is located in **Caleta de Fueste** at the Barceló hotel complex that, however, is not accessible.

Not far from the Castillo de El Tostón there is a **whale skeleton**, then the beautiful beaches start, which are one of the biggest attractions of the place. The more than 1 km long **Playa del Castillo is a** meeting point for body and kite surfers.

The small **Ermita de Nuestra Señora del Buen Viaje** is located at the northern edge of the village of El Cotillo. The simple building was built in 1834 and bears a tiny bell cage on the left side.

From El Cotillo, the coastal road leads north to the **Museo de la Pesca Tradicional**, the **Fisheries Museum**.

On this road follows the **Playa Los Lagos de Cotillo,** which is located at the end of the village.

Afterwards the popular beach, the **Playa de La Concha,** follows.

Following the road, you come to **Caleta del Rio**.

The fishing museum can already be recognized from a distance by the red and white striped lighthouse, the **Faro El Tostón**.

In 1897 construction work began on the original lighthouse with the outbuilding for the lighthouse keeper, which has since been converted into a fishing museum.

The lighthouse served as a marker of the sea area of the same name from the Ballena headland and marks the Bocaina strait between Fuerteventura and Lanzarote.

In the middle of the 20th century, due to the low height and the dilapidation of the old tower, it was decided to build a new higher lighthouse, which was inaugurated in 1955.

The new, red and white striped El Testón lighthouse is operated automatically and has a height of 30 metres. Its range is 14 nautical miles, which is about 26 km. The work required for maintenance and operation is carried out by the lighthouse keeper of the **La Entallada lighthouse,** located in the south near **Las Playitas.**

The museum is dedicated to fishing and its importance for Fuerteventura with Spanish-English panels and inscriptions. A German 30-page information booklet is provided at the entrance to understand the panels.

Opening hours: 10.00 - 17.30, closed on Sundays and Mondays.

Please note that toilets are available but cannot be used. Also the old lighthouse is no longer accessible. It is advisable to drink a cortado in the museum café or sit on the sheltered outdoor terrace to relax.

Tip: If you want to stretch your legs after a long journey, you can take a 30-minute, signposted walk around the lighthouse.

Further dreamlike bathing bays, the **Playas de Los Charcos**, are not far from the lighthouse, in northern direction.

11 Villaverde

In the centre of the village is the small church of **Ermita de San Vicente Ferrer de Villaverde**, whose main portal is at the rear.

The place would be worth a visit if the main attraction, the **Cueva del Llano** cave, were still open.

It is located on the FV-101, direction **Villaverde** and is signposted from the main road.

The cave was formed about 1 million years ago when a lava flow cooled from the outside and a lava flow flowed out from the inside. It is with 648 m the longest and biggest cave of the island and has a diameter of 7 to 10 m.

The cave has been closed since 2017, when the **spider species Maiorerus randoi,** native to Fuerteventura and threatened with extinction, lives here in the rear part, which is inaccessible to humans.

The spider species found exclusively in this cave was first discovered in 1991 and is a remarkable example of how the spider has adapted to life in absolute darkness.

The only 2.2 mm small spider, of which approximately 20 specimens still exist, is yellowish because it has lost all pigment coloration. Because of the darkness she is blind, because her eyes have receded. Their legs and antennas, which are used exclusively for orientation, are long and thin.

Genetic investigations have shown that this spider species originated in Africa, probably arrived in Fuerteventura on flotsam and has developed into independent species.

Over time, due to increasing drought on the island, probably all other species have died out, so that only the few specimens in the **Cuevas de Llanos** survived due to the constant temperatures and high humidity in the cave.

12 La Oliva

At that time **La Oliva** stood in the middle of olive groves, which led to its name. After the conquest of the Canary Islands, the military regiment headed for the island directly from La Oliva between 1708 and 1859, so that many interesting sights reflect the island's history here.
In the centre is the church of **Nuestra Señora de La Candeleria**, which is one of the largest in Fuerteventura and has undergone various transformations over the centuries.

The exact construction period is not known, but the date of origin is dated to the 17th century, from which the west portal originated.
The highlight of the five-part high altar wall is the sculpture of the **Señora de La Candeleria** with Child, a copy of the patron saint from Tenerife.
By the way: For beautiful photos, the church lighting, which is located at the entrance on the right, must be switched on for a fee.

The Casa de Los Coroneles, a house steeped in history, is signposted on the outskirts of the town, in Calle Los Coroneles.
The building is situated in front of the **volcanic mountain Montaña Oliva** with a height of 326 m. It dates from the 2nd half of the 17th century and is the largest country estate on the Canary Islands.

The military regime resided here under the leadership of the first colonel, **Señor Ginés de Cabrera Bethencourt**, who settled in La Oliva with his family in 1708. He appropriated vast estates and gained more and more political influence, so that he owned almost a third of the island.
The huge estate with patio was once said to have a window for every day, 365, but in reality it's "only" 117. Since the farmers couldn't read, write or calculate, they tried to express the size and their fascination for the building in this way.

Until 1994 the manor house was owned by the community of heirs of the descendants of Colonel Bethencourt. It was bought by the island government and restored from 2001 to 2006.

Opening hours: Tuesdays to Saturdays: 10.00 - 18.00, Mondays, Sundays and public holidays closed. Tel.: 0034 928 868 280 Admission: 3,00 €.

The Ermita de Puerto Rico is inconspicuous, but steeped in history. It is located on the right side, in the side street before the Casa de Coronel.
It was the first chapel built in La Oliva to express the deep Christian faith of the villagers.

The beautiful stonemasonry work on the door and window surrounds, which show geometric and vegetable ornaments in light sand-lime brick, is striking. Not far from the church is the **grain museum of La Cilla**. Since cereals and pulses played a very important role for the majos, the grain museum was housed in the **Casa de La Cilla**, the former grain store. It is located in Calle La Orilla. In Cillas were stored the harvest entries of the church, which came from own property and from centab levies. Further granaries were located in Betancuria, Tiscamanita, Tetir and Tindaya.
The building was built at the beginning of the 19th century in the style of traditional island architecture and restored by the Island Council. Agricultural equipment will be exhibited and farming procedures will be explained to give an insight into the life of the rural population.
History: Traditional farming on Fuerteventura: Farming was the most important economic activity on the island, which the Majos pursued until the middle of the last century before the conquest of the island. First, the fertile valleys and plains of the island were divided into lands and populated so that the food supply of the islanders, the social structure and trade could be ensured.
The main crops were wheat, barley, rye, pulses, maize and fruit trees.
In rainy years the harvest was very successful, so that considerable quantities could be sold. However, the island turned into a poorhouse in years of low rainfall, without any significant crop yields.
The everyday life of the population was primarily concerned with the cultivation of grain. The rainwater had to be collected and the soil prepared for cultivation and sowing.
Due to the constant lack of water, the farmers developed special techniques to use the precious water as well as possible when it rains.

In Fuerteventura it has always been customary to regard rainwater as a public good, which was used along natural watercourses that could not be interrupted.

The harvest was generally harvested between March and June, depending on rainfall, sowing and planting season. First barley and lentils were harvested, then the remaining legumes and wheat.

It was carried out by the peasant family or groups of farm workers, which consisted of neighbours or relatives. Depending on the effort, wage earners were also employed, who were paid with money or a proportion of grain.

The workers' food, which was at the farmer's expense, consisted of mojo sauces, bread, gofio, figs, salted fish, and water and wine were available as drinks.

As the display boards of the exhibition are exclusively inscribed in Spanish, one gets a booklet with German explanations at the cash desk.

Admission: 1,50 € Opening hours: Tuesdays to Fridays 10.00 - 17.00 hrs.

Not far from the **Casa de Los Coroneles**, the **Centro de Arte Canario- Casa Mané** is located in the Calle Salvador Manrique de Lara.

The centre was created in 1991 by the private initiative of the **art dealer Manuel Delgado Camino,** who was called **Mané**, in which over 80 artists exhibited their works.

Opening hours: Mondays to Fridays 10.00 - 17.00, Saturdays 10.00 - 14.00. Admission: 5,00 €. Phone: 0034 928 868 233/ 0034 616 531 930

By the way: As an art lover, one should plan half a day for the extensive exhibition.

One last testimony of prosperity, the **Casa del Inglés**, is located on the side of the road that leads from **La Oliva** to Villaverde.

The **Casa del Inglés** is an 18th century building also called Sitio de Don David, the seat of Mr David.

It is an important example of the architecture of the rural bourgeoisie and presented its economic power in La Oliva.

The builder, Señor Julian Leal Sicilia, whose family came from La Palma, dedicated himself to agriculture and trade between the Canary Islands and America.

Originally the house had 2 floors and an inner courtyard with an Aljibe, a water reservoir. Two partition walls divided the object into a north and south wing. Financial losses in his commercial activities forced Señor Sicilia to sell his house, which became the property of the English naturalist Mr. David Parkinson, who dedicated himself to the flora and fauna of the island.

Since the population remembered after years only that an Englishman lived in the house, the ruin carries the name Casa del Inglés, the house of the Englishman.

When Mr. Parkinson returned to his homeland, he sold the house, which was used differently afterwards. During the Guerra Civil, the Spanish Civil War, it was occupied by the army and served as a hospital for the armed forces located in La Oliva.

Tip: La Oliva Entrance- Combi- Ticket: With this ticket, which must be bought locally in **La Oliva**, you can visit the grain museum **La Cilla**, the **Casa de Coroneles** and the **Casa Mané**. The ticket can be purchased at all 3 sights and costs €6.00 instead of €9.50. All you have to do is ask at an entrance ticket office.

Tip: If you are on holiday in the north of the island, you should join the guided tour, which starts at 10.00 a.m.

A highlight for authentic souvenirs is the **Mercado de las Tradiciones.**

The market is located in the **Casa del Coronel**, in Calle Francisco Fuentes Martín, 15 Tuesdays and Fridays between 10.00 and 14.00 hours homemade crafts and food are offered.

13 Tindaya

The 400 m high **Montaña de Tindaya** is the holy mountain of the natives, the **Guanches** of Fuerteventura, on which they possessed a cult and burial place. The biggest attraction are the more than 200 rock carvings, in the form of foot contours of the Guanches.

Due to repeated vandalism and careless wanderers, many of the carvings were irretrievably destroyed, so that the island government has imposed an absolute ban on climbing the Tindaya.

Since even after long protests by nature conservationists the mining of the volcanic rock for house building was stopped, the quarrying sites of the quarry can still be clearly seen on the slope of the Tindaya.

At the edge of the village entrance, after the Centro Cultural, there is a small chapel with an open bell cage made of black stone.
At the end of the village, slightly elevated, lies the cheese dairy **Quesos de Tindaya**, where goat cheese is offered from Monday to Saturday in the time from 08.30 to 14.00 o'clock.

The restored building **Casa Alta de Tindaya** is not far from the FV-10 and is dedicated to the late **artist** and sculptor **Eduardo Chillida**.
It was planned to drill two long vertical light shafts into the volcanic mountain Tindaya and to connect them with an already existing tunnel, which was to serve as access. The shafts should be located on the front and rear side of the mountain to present the visitor with the different play of light of sun and moon. Although the project was planned on the opposite side of the rock carvings, it was not implemented.

In the first exhibition room, two columns of shaft models are used to simulate the play of light.
In the second room, a large wooden model of the volcano mountain illustrates the artist's intentions, and several excavated stone blocks with rock carvings are shown.
The exhibition is completed by film screenings, which also take place on the upper floor.
Open: Tuesdays to Sundays from 10.00 - 14.00. Admission free.

On the left above the **Casa Alta de Tindaya**, directly beside the main road, a gravel road leads to the monument of the Spanish **poet Unamuno**, to the **Monumento Unamuno**.
On the occasion of its 100th birthday, the island's government erected a monument to the great Spanish poet and poet Miguel Unamuno in the volcanic mountain of Montañas Quemada, not far from Tindaya. The mountain was chosen because Unamuno described in one of his letters to a trusted friend that this region was one of the places where he would like to be buried after his death.

14 Casas de Filipito

The complex **Casas de Filipito** is located at the FV-10 Puerto del Rosario, direction Tetír. At **La Asomada**, take the FV-219 towards **El Time**.

Follow the signs and after about 15 minutes you reach the **Casas de Felipito** on a gravel road.

The finca is located in the Llano del Triguero, the plain of the grain, which got its name because of the cultivation of grain.

It was named after **Felipe Ruíz Gonzáles**, who was called Felipito el feo- the small, ugly Philipp, a farmer who lived here with his parents at the beginning of the 20th century.

The two-storey dwelling house is located directly at the entrance on the right and shows a typical dwelling house where modest farmers lived.

After its restoration, the complex was opened as a museum in 2002 and is used by islanders as a kind of leisure park with covered, wind-protected seating, barbecue areas, children's playground and bowling alleys.

The remarkable thing about the plant are the efforts the farmer made to cultivate and make fertile a land interspersed with limestone. He used the limestones to build walls as wind shelters and as enclosures for animals up to 3 m high. He designed drainage systems to carry rainwater to his property. He had the dubious honour of being the first majorero to die in the Viejo Hospital in the old hospital, now the University of Fuerteventura.

Opening hours: Wednesdays to Sundays from 10.30- 18.00. Admission is free.

15 Puertito de los Molinos

The FV-221 leads past a wide gorge which, in rainy seasons, leads the water from the volcanic mountains into the sea to **Puerto de los Molinos.** After heavy rainfall the area is beautifully green, but in summer the play of colours fades.

Arrived in the village, you have the possibility to leave your car and cross a bridge under which ducks have settled to get to 2 restaurants.

But the most beautiful view over the bay is if you walk up the path to the left of the parking lot.

The dark stone pebble beach at **Playa los Molinos** is not suitable as a bathing beach due to the tides and waves.

16 Tetír

The small village is located on the FV-10, at the height of Puerto del Rosario. The seven-storey bell tower of the **Santo Domingo de Guzmán parish church** can be seen from afar.

The church dates back to the 18th century and was placed under a preservation order after renovation work that revealed old murals from this period.

The Gofio Museum is located directly on the main street. The owner of the museum, Mr. Francisco Cabrera Oramas, is the last active gofio miller in the world.

Gofio is a flour made from roasted corn. It was the staple food in the Canary Islands.

Behind the museum you can watch how corn is roasted.

It is a pity that the miller only speaks Spanish and only demonstrates the grinding of the maize grains when larger travel groups come to the museum.

Nevertheless, you should buy a bag of real gofio flour here, as it was not industrially produced.

Opening hours: Tuesdays to Fridays 9.00 - 14.00, 16.30 - 19.30, Saturdays 10.00 - 17.00, Sundays 10.00 - 15.00. **Tip:** Call the hotel reception at 639 752 848 in the museum to find out when the miller is grinding the gofio.

17 Tefia

The open air museum **Ecomuseo La Alcogida** is located at the FV- 207 in **Tefía** and is the main attraction of the village.

In the first small white building complex next to the car park there is the reception, where you can buy tickets and get a plan of the tour.

The museum is a reconstruction of a traditional rural village. It consists of 7 representative houses that have been faithfully restored with materials used by the Majoreros.

For the most part, the houses have 2 floors and flat, or sloping roof areas with Arabic roof tiles. From very complex constructions where wealthy families lived, to simple buildings reminiscent of the modest conditions of the peasants of Fuerteventura, you can find a wide range of buildings.

The village was inhabited until the 70s of the last century, and was restored by the island government from 1992.

Each house has received the name of its original owners; the house of Señora Hermina and Señor Donato shows simple living conditions.

The houses have a U-shaped or L-shaped ground plan, the inner courtyard faces south to protect it from strong winds and is closed by a wall.

In the case of the wealthy families, several outbuildings were arranged around the inner courtyard, which were accessed by a wooden or stone staircase. The wealth was expressed, among other things, in small roofed balconies and surrounding wooden galleries on the upper floor.

In the houses of the Herrera and Cabra families, as well as of the miller, the Molino family, the traditional craftsmanship of the island lives on.

In the rooms there are basket weavers, potters, weavers, embroiderers and stonemasons whose articles are offered for sale.

Opening hours: Tuesdays to Saturdays 10.00 - 18.00, admission: 5,00 €.

At the entrance to the village there is a windmill of the **Molina** type, opposite which a road leads to the eastern part of the village to the **Ermita de Tefía,** surrounded by a high wall.

The church dates from the early 18th century and was placed under monument protection. To the left is the arena for the **Lucha Canaria**, the Canarian wrestling match.

18   Puerto del Rosario

The history of the **island's capital**: The former anchorage for merchant ships was already listed on a Venetian nautical chart in 1426 and served primarily as a loading point for goats, which were taken on the voyage as living provisions for the crew of the large merchant ships. For this reason, the port was called **Puerto de Cabras** from the 18th century, translated as **goat port.**

In the 19th century the English used the port as a base to control trade with Gran Canaria and mainland Europe. In 1806, Puerto de Cabras left his mother's parish in Tetír and chose the Madonna of the Rosary, the **Virgen del Rosario,** as patron saint of her own parish church, and in 1835 she declared herself an independent parish. In 1860 the port city, where the trade with soda, lime, goats and the red dye from the Koschenille louse breeding flourished, was appointed the **island capital.** It was not until 1956 that the city was allowed to rename itself **Puerto del Rosario** after the name of its patron saint.

Places of interest: The parish church of **Nuestra Señora del Rosario** is located in the historic centre of the city, between **Calle León y Castillo** and **Avenida 1 de Mayo**.

It was built in 1812 and was the first religious building in the centre of the island. It was a small house of prayer dedicated to the Virgin of El Rosario. In the years 1824-1835 the central bell tower was added, which is today integrated in the east facade. The wrought-iron, ornate lattices on the main portal are conspicuous. In the middle of the high altar is the patron saint of the church with the Child Jesus on her arm. Every year, on 7 October, a festival is held in honour of the Nuestra Señora del Rosario. On this occasion the main portal is opened and the processional figures are carried through the streets together with the Madonna.

The museum **Casa Museo Unamuno** is located in **Calle Virgen del Rosario**, opposite the church.
The building was registered in 1877 in the land register of **Puerto de Cabras**, the original name of Puerto del Rosario. At that time it was a small guesthouse, called "Hotel Fuerteventura", where the Spanish writer **Miguel de Unamuno** lived on the island for 5 months during his exile. The museum is a testimony of the typical architecture of Canarian houses from that time.

Opening hours: Open daily from 09.00 - 14.00, closed on Saturdays, Sundays and public holidays. Admission is free.

Additional information:
Miguel de Unamuno was professor and rector of the Spanish University in Salamanca. On 12 March 1924 he was banished to Fuerteventura by the then head of state because of critical statements against the regime.
He lived 5 months on the island in exile, made me friends with the inhabitants and wrote down his impressive impressions about Fuerteventura, which were published in daily newspapers in Madrid, Buenos Aires and Gran Canaria.

He then voluntarily fled to France to take up his fight outside Spain against the dictatorship.

On his 100th birthday, the island government erected a monument to him on the **Montaña Quemada**, not far from the village of **Tindaya**.
The Art Museum **Centro de Arte Juan Ismael** is located a little away from the harbour, in Calle Alimirante Lallemand, 30, opposite the petrol station.
From Tuesday to Saturday, Canarian and international works of art as well as objects by Juan Ismael will be exhibited on several floors between 9.00 and 13.00 and 17.00 and 21.00 hours.
Tip: To make sure that an exhibition is also taking place and that you are not standing in front of empty walls, call 928 859 750/ 51/ 52 to confirm the exhibition.

18.1 Shopping in Puerto del Rosario
The largest shopping center on the island, the Centro Comercial **Las Rotondas**, is located at the roundabout of Calle Francisco Pi y Arsuaga.
Opening hours: Mondays- Saturdays from 10.00- 22.00, Sundays closed. You can find all information about the current brand shops at: www.lasrotondascentrocomercial.com

The small market hall of the **Mercado Municipal** is located below the centre, towards the port, in the Calle Teófilo Martinez Escobar not far from the **Plaza España**.
From Monday to Friday, from 7.00 a.m. to 1.00 p.m., traders offer a selection of fruit, vegetables, meat, fish and cheese.
Tip: Visit this small market with the friendly sellers while it is still possible.
Due to a small number of visitors, it could be foreseeable that this small market hall will no longer exist permanently.

The **Mercado Agrario de Fuerteventura** is located on the upper floor of the central bus station, the **Estación de Guagas**, in the Avenida la Constitución. On Saturdays from 8.00 to 14.00 we offer homemade products and food.

18.2 Beaches in Puerto del Rosario

The city beach of Puerto del Rosario, the **Playa Chica**, is located on the **Avenida de los Reyes de España** and not far from the ferry and commercial port.
South of the capital is **Playa Blanca, a** long white sandy beach signposted by the FV-2 motorway.

Interesting: **Graffiti art -** the new facades of the capital city
In January 2011, the Planning Office of **Puerto del Rosario** decided to have the dilapidated facades of the capital's buildings beautified.
After consultation with the owners, a competition for artistic design, the "**Concurso de Arte Urbano de Puerto de Rosario**", was announced in 2015. In the meantime more than 36 artists were allowed to realize their works.
Due to positive feedback from islanders and tourists this project will be continued.

1 LA NARADORA- The swimmer, quarter: Los Pozos, artist: Dailos Paniagua Rodriguez, year: 2013, address: Calle Hibiscos, 4
2 LAS CHICAS DEL PUENTE- The Girls of the Bridge, Quarter: Los Pozos, Artist: Luis de Dios, Year: 2013, Address: Rotondas de acceso al Hospital- Circle- Direction Hospital
3 BALLENAS AZULES- Blue whales, quarter: Los Pozos, artist: Derque Catellano Femandez, year: 2015, address: Carretera a los Pozos, 26
4 SIRENO, district: Los Pozos, artist: Nazaret Umpierrez del Rio, year: 2015, address: Calle Secundino Alonso corner Calle Puerto Cabras
5 ABUBILLAS- Wiederhopf, quarter: Centro, artist: Laura Perera Castro, year: 2015, address: Calle Hermanos Machado,22
6 LA GRAN MANZANA- The Big Apple, Quarter: Centro, Artist: Luis E. Jimenez Deniz, year: 2014, address: Calle Secundino Alonso, 50
7 PROSPECCIÓN DIGITAL- Digital prospection, quarter: Centro, artist: Angel Moran Romero, year: 2014, address: Calle Juan Tadeo Cabrera, 30
8 CULTIVA EL CORAZON- heart cultivation, quarter: Centro, artist: Dena Martin Soler, year: 2013, address: Calle Secundino Alonso corner Calle Juan Tadeo Cabrera

9 PALMAR- palm forest, quarter: Centro, artist: Paula Calavera Candela, year: 2015, address: Calle Primero de Mayo, 47

10 FOLCLORE DE HOY- Today's folklore, quarter: Centro, artist: Ione Domingez Luis, year: 2015, address: Calle Primero de Mayo, 74

11 ATARDECER EN SERENGUETY- Dusk in the Serengeti, quarter: Centro, artist: Derque Catellano Fernandez, year: 2015, address: Torreta Calle Primero de Mayo (Barranco Pilón)

12 ABRIENDO MENTES, CERRANDO ESTIGMAS- Opening the senses, closing the wounds, quarter: Centro, artist: Sofia Lorenzo Mederos, year: 2014, address: Calle Jesus y Maria corner Calle Santo Tomas de Aquino

13 REGISTRO DE VIENTO- Wind directory, quarter: Centro, artist: Giorgos Garth Chistou, year: 2015, address: City. Library, Calle Santo Tomas de Aquino

14 JUSTICIA- Justice
Quarter: Centro, Artist: Juan Pedro Mendoza Vera, Year: 2013, Address: Calle Primero de Mayo Corner Calle José Diaz Diaz

15 EVOLUCION= EDUCACION- Evolution= Education, Quarter: Majada Marcial, Artist: Maria de la Peña Gutierrez, Year: 2015, Address: Backside CEIP Agustin Millares Carlo/ Calle Manuel Velazquez Cabrera

16 NUNCA MAS? - Never? Quarter: El Charco, Artist: Angel Moran Romero, Year: 2015, Address: Calle Hernan Cortes, 84

17 CETACEOPELIN, district: El Charco, artist: Francisco Perdomo Feo, year: 2015, address: Calle Alfonso XVIII, 44

18 PUEBLO COSTERO- coastal village, district: El Charco, artist: Sofia Lorenzo Mederos, year: 2013, address: Calle Almirante Lallemand, 127

19 EL PESCAO HABLADOR- The talkative fish, quarter: El Charco, artist: Sabotaje al Montaje, year: 2014, address: Calle Comandante Diaz Trayter, 55

20 ORQUESTA orchestras, quarter: Majada Marcial, artist: Zebenzui Armas, year: 2014, address: Calle Los Canteros, 18

21 LA NOVELERA- The fantasist, quarter: La Charca, artist: Dailos Paniagua, year: 2013, address: Calle Socrates, 17

22 DAR ES AMAR- Giving is love, quarter: La Charca, artist: Luis de Dios, year: 2013, address: Calle Juan de Bethencourt, 48

23 ESTACION DE FERROCARRIL- railway station, district: La Charca, artist: Dailos Paniagua, year: 2014, address: Block of houses Calle Juan de Bethencourt / Calle Secundino Delgado

24 AFRICA CALL- Africaruf, district: Buenavista, artist: Corinna, year: 2014, address: Calle Gomera, 5

25 GUIRRE- Adler, quarter: Fabelo, artist: Angel Moran Romero, year: 2015, address: Calle Isla Graciosa, 3

26 LA APANADA- The Skillful, Quarter: Fabelo, Artist: Derque Castellano Fernandey, Year: 2015, Address: Calle Castilla, 36

27 PAREJA- couples, quarter: Fabelo, artist: Sabotaje al Montaje, year: 2015, address: Calle Maria Estrada corner Calle Castilla

28 ESCADERAS AL CIELO- staircase to heaven, quarter: Fabelo, artist: Doris Alessio, year: 2015, address: Calle La Gavia- School- Colegio Pablo Neruda

29 BAZUR2V1SU2, quarter: Fabelo, artist: Francisco Perdomo Feo, year: 2015, address: Calle Maria Estrada Corner Calle Palmera Canaria

30 SAHARA, district: Buenavista, artist: Sofia Mederos Lorenzo, year: 2015, address: Plaza Fernando Segaseta, Rocinante Street

31 ESPANTA DINOSAURIO- Dinosaur outbreak, district: Buenavista, artist: Juan Pedro Mendoza Vera, year: 2013, address: Calle La Venta, 31

32 CASA CANARIA- Canarian house, quarter: Buenavista, artist: M. Taunasu Aleman Ramirez, year: 2015, address: Carretera de Antigua, 20

33 MIRROR'S CHAMBER (El cuarto de las Maravillas)- Space of miracles,
Quarter: Tamogan, Artist: Corinna, Year: 2014, Address: Terreon de Tamogan (near the old cemetery "Cementerio viejo")

34 VIEJAS POST MODERNAS- Postmodern fish, quarter: Puerto Lajas, artist: Blas. Jose Ignacio, Blasco Rodriguez, year: 2015,
Address: Calle El Marte, 2

35 DE LA MAR- From the sea, district: Puerto Lajas, artist: Derque Catellano, year: 2015, address: Calle El Valbanera Corner Calle Los Correillos

36 MADRE AFRICA- Mother Africa
Quarter: El Matorral, Artist: José Marhenda Victoria, Year: 2014,

Address: Calle La Apañada, 50

19 Caleta de Fueste

The holiday resort **Caleta de Fuestes** is only a stone's throw from the airport to the south. Already after 7 km you reach the holiday resort, which was founded in the 1980's, and which is primarily characterized by English people.

The place, which was created on the drawing board, consists of a collection of holiday apartments and hotels, paired with small shopping centres and countless restaurants.

A long promenade leads directly along the big, artificially arranged, snow-white main beach, the **Playa Caleta de Fuestes Beach.**
Worth seeing and giving the place its name is the defensive tower that dates back to the year 1740 and stands at the promenade in front of the Barceló hotel complex and is identical in construction with the **Castillo de El Tostón** in **El Cotillo.** With these towers the coasts were protected from the frequent attacks by pirates, English and French.

Markets:
The popular **Africa Market** is located on the main road FV-2 directly above the roundabout, and takes place on Tuesdays and Saturdays from 10.00 - 14.00 hrs.

20 Playa La Guirra

South of **Caleta de Fuestes** lies the holiday resort **Playa La Guirra**, to which Fuerteventura's first 18-hole golf course belongs. Opposite, on the sea side, there are large hotels and the **shopping centre Centro Comercial Atlantico.**
The promenade begins at the centre, where several lime kilns from bygone times can be seen. From here you can walk to **Caleta de Fuestes.**
Current shops and opening hours of the **Centro Comercial Atlantico** at:
www.ccatlanticofuerteventura.com

21 Salinas del Carmen

The Saltmuseum **Museo de la Sal** is located on the FV-2 south of **Caleta de Fuestes**.

The complex consists of 2 complexes: The main building houses a permanent exhibition on the history of salt and the

Salinas del Carmen, built around 1910. The tour begins to the left of the building complex.

1 Saltadero: This is the highest point of the salt flats. The wind drives the waves to the rocks and on impact foam is formed in which the salt concentration is highest. The water collects in the collecting basin and is passed on.

2 Cocederos: The collected water flows through a channel into further collecting basins.

3 Tajos: When the water arrives at the Cocedero, it evaporates and the salt crystallizes. A thin film of salt forms on the surface, which is removed twice a day so that the salt can settle on the ground. As soon as the water has almost completely evaporated, the salt worker skims the salt from the bottom and lets it drip off to the side. It is then collected and taken to the warehouse.

4 Almacen: This is where the salineros' tools are stored, the cleaned and dried salt is stored and packed in bags.

5 Embarcadero loading bay: From El Muellito, the small quay, the salt was loaded in wagons for shipment to the other Canary Islands.

6 Horno de Cal- lime kilns: Lime was needed for the construction and maintenance of the salt works. In the period from October to March, when no salt could be extracted, lime was burned in the kilns. The stone oven has 2 lateral chambers to store limestone and burnt lime.

7 Aljibe cistern: The cistern is located in a small valley where water was collected for the supply of the finca.

Open: Tuesday to Friday and Sunday from 9.30 to 17.30, entrance fee: 5,00 € per person.

22 Malpais Grande

The coastal road between **Pozo Negro** and **Gran Tarajal** leads through the **Malpais grande**, a volcanic landscape covered with large and small volcanic boulders. This region is so called, because after extreme volcanic eruptions, the area was difficult for the natives to pass.

23 Pozo Negro

The small fishing village of **Pozo Negro is** located at the end of the FV-420, and the route goes through the **Malpais Grande**, the "big bad land" created by the eruptions of the **volcanoes Caldera de La Laguna** and **Caldera de Liria**.

In the 15th century the town was one of the most important ports on the island due to its natural harbour. Meanwhile it has become very quiet around Pozo Negro with its 2 small fish restaurants.

The actual sight, the **open-air museum**, the **Centro de Interpretacion Poblado de La Atalayita**, is only a few kilometres before Pozo Negro.

A bumpy path leads to the interpretation centre, which is half underground in the earth. On display are photos and texts on flora, fauna and the indigenous people, the majos, Fuerteventuras.

To the village **La Atalayita** it goes, below the parking lot, on foot.

The village is named after the elevated volcanic cone of **Lomo de Atalayita**, which the aborigines used as a lookout point for surveillance of the coastal section of Pozo Negro.

Life essentially took place outdoors, inhabiting small circular structures of stacked lava stones. There were different indigenous settlements, some lasting for generations, others only as hiding places in the face of the invasions of the conquerors.

La Atalayita occupies an area of 45,000 square meters, on which 115 buildings with partly different structures can be found.

At the entrance to the village, a building has been restored that reflects the traditional architecture of the island and the local architecture. In contrast to the old buildings, the ground plan is rectangular, the roof consists of a rod and bar construction on which clay is applied. On the side of this house there are remains of shells of shells and snails, whose meat, after fish, was the most important source of food and from which simple tools were made.

The houses of the Majos have different structures. They have a diameter of 1.50- 2.00 m and a circular or elliptical ground plan. The entrance is narrow and low. There are also connected residential complexes with outbuildings that open onto a central square surrounded by walls. Here, areas separated by stone walls, shepherd dogs, sheep and camels were kept. They also used volcanic lava grottos as living space, which were accessed through a narrow wall opening with two descending steps.

Admission is free and the Visitor Centre is now permanently closed. By the way: the covered benches in front of the interpretation centre invite you to take a break for lunch or a breather.

24 Tuineje

In the centre of the village of **Tuineje** is the **church of San Miguel Arcangel**.

The villagers are proud of the battle successfully waged against the English on **Tamasite** in 1740. This was depicted in two panel paintings on the right and left of the altar pedestal.

The Battle of Tamasite: Due to the discovery of America, the Canary Islands conquered by the Spanish crown became the most important stopover for a safe passage across the Atlantic.

In order to assert its claims on the Canary Islands, the English royal family declared war on Spain in 1730. However, only 10 years later, on 12 October 1740, 50 heavily armed English corsairs arrived in the port of Gran Tarajal to conquer the then capital Betancuria.

From Gran Tarajal they came, direction Tuineje, through the dry gorges well forward without being discovered.

According to legend, on 13 October the English invaded the settlement of Casillas Blanca, south of Tamasite, forcing a farmer to lead them to the commander in Betancuria. However, he was still able to get one of his sons to walk over the 346 m high mountain of Tamasite in time to alert the inhabitants of Tuineje, so that the church bells could be rung immediately from village to village.

When the English reached Tuineje and plundered the church, they had already noticed that the inhabitants had stood up and approached help from the surrounding villages, so that they decided to retreat towards the sea.

The commander of the Majoreros asked for the help of the patron saint San Miguel and ordered the farmers to round up their dromedaries in order to oppose the English south of Tamasite at the pass of El Cuchillo.

The dromedaries find the hail of bullets, so that the peasants emerged victorious from this battle. They made an oath to their patron saint, which was forgotten in the course of time.

About 200 years later, in 1946, the clergyman of Tuineje reminded the inhabitants of the historical battle and declared October 13 as a feast day, which was put into practice in 1974.

25 Pájara

Already in the 16th century shepherds and fishermen settled here and founded **Pájara**, which today is one of the oldest places on the island.

Worth seeing is the church **Nuestra Señora de la Regla**, whose construction began in 1645 and was completed in 1687. In the 18th century it was extended by the right side aisle. The striking stonemasonry work on the portal, which is Aztec-inspired and looks like snakes, feathers, suns and lions, comes from local artists who probably took ideas and inspiration from Italian reference books.

If you want to see the dark interior of the church illuminated, you are asked to pay 1,00 € for 6 minutes.
Not far from the church there is a restored **Noria**, a water fountain that was once used by camels and is now still used as a tourist attraction by a donkey.

26 Ajuy

The FV-621 leads directly to a small fishing village **Ajuy**, also called **Puerto de la Peña.** The 10 km long stretch of coast was declared a **natural monument Monumento Natural** in 1994 because of its important history for the island and the impressive limestone formations.

Once you arrive in the village, you can park at the designated car park above the fishing village or drive to the 2nd car park directly on the beach.

The black, fine sandy beach is open for swimming depending on the season, but should be viewed with great caution due to the extreme undercurrents. Not for nothing is it called **Playa de Los Muertos**, the beach of the dead, but its name still comes from the time of the conquistadors, when the pirates caused a terrible bloodbath to the natives here. To explore the highlights of Ajuy, a path leads up to the right of the beach.

Information about the lime kilns can be found along the way. Then the trail leads to a viewing platform, downhill via steps you can explore the cave inside the volcano, which served as a hiding place from pirates.

Also the way back offers a fantastic view over the whole coastline, beautiful photos are included.

27 Vega de Río Palmas

From **Pájara** the FV-30 runs towards **Betancuria**. The winding route leads past mountain peaks up to 700 m high and offers views as far as the sea.

Shortly after the road sign "**Degollada de los Granadillos**" there is the 1st viewing platform, the **Mirador del Risco de la Peña**.
On the way you come to the 2nd vantage point, the **Mirador Las Peñitas**, with a view of the dam surrounded by palm trees. Due to bad planning, one can only speak of a reservoir after rainy times.
When you arrive in the village, you have the possibility to drive to the palm covered beginning of the reservoir. Turn left at the end of the village and follow the road.
At the end of the road that leads to **Casa de la Naturaleza**, turn left.

Drivers are not allowed to enter the reservoir due to a private barrier. Here are planted cactus fig cacti. On closer inspection, one first assumes a mould infestation.

However, this is a **Koschinellen breeding**. Originating in Mexico, the louse bred on the cactus plant produces a carmine that has been used since the Aztecs for dyeing fabrics, food and cosmetics. In 1835 she arrived in Lanzarote and Fuerteventura. The cactus shoots are planted in April and, when they are large enough, are infected by insects. In summer they are harvested carefully with tin spoons. The process of drying and cleaning to obtain the cochineal is meticulous and strictly traditional. Since the red dye was produced artificially, however, the breeding lost importance.
At the end of the village, towards Betancuria, there is the **Virgen de La Peña** Sanctuary.

The impressive church is open daily from 10.30 am to 3.15 pm. The fair takes place on Sundays at 12.00 o'clock.

28 Betancuria

The **Betancuria Nature Park** is the largest on the island with over 100 square kilometres and covers 10% of the total island area.

The former island capital has a long and interesting history.

After the expulsion of the natives, 1404 European settlers found a safe place to settle in the valley, which at that time was still very rich in water. The French nobleman and knight **Jean de Béthencourt** had conquered Fuerteventura in the twinkling of an eye from Lanzarote on behalf of his king Henry III. When he founded his first town on the island, he simply named the place after his surname - this is how Béthencourt became **Betancuria**.

The conqueror had embarked and settled over 200 craftsmen and farmers from Normandy in order to quickly establish a functioning structure in the city.

In 1593 Berber pirates, under the leadership of the feared leader **Xabán de Arráez** Betancuria, attacked and almost completely razed them to the ground. But already in the same year the reconstruction works of the city and the cathedral began, which were completed only in 1691.

At that time, feudal residences were mainly built, which were gradually abandoned when, in 1835, **Puerto de Cabras**, now **Puerto del Rosario**, became the capital of the island.

The sights of the place are under monument protection.

Coming from the signposted car park, one gets upstairs to the main street of the village.

If you follow the road towards the church, you will find a city map on the right-hand side to help you find your way around.

The church of **Santa Maria de Betancuria** is located at the back of the village.

Since the **Museum of Sacred Art** is located in the rear left part of the church, the church entrance fee is 1,50 €. Opening hours: Monday - Saturday: 10.00 - 12.30 and 13.00 - 15.50, Sunday: 10.30 - 14.20.

In the building next to the church there is a large souvenir shop.

In the same complex, but at the back of the souvenir shop, is the **Centro Insular de Artesanía**, a combination of exhibition centre and film screening. Entrance fee: 6,00 €.

First one is led into a hall, in which photo impressions about Fuerteventura are shown. In the 2nd room a 3-D film about the underwater world of the island is shown.

Afterwards you can have a look at the exhibition in the inner courtyard.

The garden area leads to a café/restaurant with terrace, which is also accessible from the street.

Just before leaving Betancuria, in the direction of **Mirador de Morro Velosa**, a path on the right leads to the ruins of the **Convent Church of San Buenaventura**.

On the left entrance side of the ruin, a small marble plaque commemorates the Spanish conqueror Diego García de Herrera, who chose Fuerteventura as the starting point for his slave trade and was buried in the monastery in 1485.

Shortly after the Spanish crown conquered the island, the construction of the **Franciscan monastery** began in 1416, the first in the Canary Islands from which missionaries Christianized the population.

Opposite the ruin is the **Ermita San Diego**, which can be reached through a wall opening.

According to tradition, there was a small cave in which the **Franciscan monk Diego de Alcalá,** abbot of the monastery from 1445 to 1449, retired.

After his death in 1463, a small chapel was built above the cave, from which elements were used to build the present Ermita, which was completed in the 17th century.

The Mirador **de Guise y Ayose** is located at the FV-30, on the way to the **Mirador de Morro Velosa**.

The impressive 4.50m high statues present **Ayose, King of Jandía** and **Guise, King of Maxorata**.

Fuerteventura was called Erbania by the natives. Until the arrival of the European conquerors in 1402, led by the French **Jean de Bethencourt** and **Gadifer de la Salle**, the island was divided into two kingdoms at **Istmo de La Pared**, the isthmus of **La Pared:** Maxorata in the north and Jandía in the south. The enemy kings surrendered without a fight to their enemies and were baptized. The baptisms took place on 18 and 28 January 1405, with which they received the new names Luis and Alfonso.

29 Mirador de Morro Velosa

The viewpoint **Morro de Velosa** is located at the FV-30, above the former island capital Betancuria, coming from Antigua, at the FV-416, direction Betancuria.

From almost every location in the centre of the island, one can see from a distance a small house that stands on the 645 m high volcanic mountain Tegú.

The Mirador was designed by the Lanzarote artist César Manrique (1919-1992) in the style of a Canarian mansion and completed in 1997.

In the building there is an exhibition on flora, fauna and history of the island, in the basement handmade souvenirs typical for the island are offered.

But the highlight is the fantastic view through the large windows to the landscape.

30 La Ampuyenta

The sleepy village lies on the FV-20 between **Casillas de Angel** and **Antigua**. On the main thoroughfare there is a large building that was built as a **hospital, San Conrado Hospital and San Gaspar Hospital,** but was never used as such. At the moment it houses the tourist information.

Free guided tours with guides to the attractions of the village start from here.

The tour starts at the back of the hospital and leads to the **Ermita de San Pedro de Alcantara** behind.

Then we cross the street, past a simple original house, to the birthplace of **Frailito Andres**.

Afterwards the house, the Casa **Museo Doctor Mena**, is approached, which lies directly at through road.

The tour ends in the **hospital** to see the premises.

Guided tours: Tuesday to Saturday at 10.30/ 12.30/ 14.30 and 16.00 hrs.

Annoying: For the new edition 2019 I checked again if the tour I did in June 2017 still takes place. The guides were currently discontinued due to a lack of demand. To gain access to Dr. Mena's church and house, have someone at your hotel reception call to make sure that the tourist information desk is open so that you can be given the keys to the tour. Tel: Mon - Fri between 08.00 and 15.00 o'clock under the number: 928 85 89 98.

30.1 Life of the Doctor Mena

Background information on the eventful life of **Doctor Mena, who** shaped the town of **Ampuyenta**: **Tomas Antonio de San Pedro Mena Mesa,** known as Doctor Mena, was born in Ampuyenta on 20 February 1802 and was christened a few weeks later, on 12 March 1802, in the church of Santa Ana in Casillas del Angel.

The modestly living family sold 10 units of barley to send their son to a school in Las Palmas because there were neither schools nor teachers in the county.

In 1820, at the age of 18, he refused to become professor at the chair of philosophy and travelled to Havana to see his brother, the priest Don Conrado. According to legend, he arrived in the port city only with a shirt and a handkerchief.

In order to begin his medical studies, Doctor Mena had to prove that he was not of Moorish, Jewish, heretical, or prosecuted descent. This was confirmed by a couple who came from Fuerteventura and knew their parents.

On 25 March 1825 Mena graduated in medicine and surgery.

Convinced that he still had much to learn, he travelled to Paris. During his 6-year stay he visited hospitals, studied medical books and acquired extensive knowledge.

He then returned to Havana, opened a practice, cared for jaundice and cholera patients and made a name for himself as a doctor and surgeon.

On 1 July 1846 he got the chair of the Faculty of Medicine and Surgery in Cadiz.

At the age of 45, he left everything behind and returned to Fuerteventura with his colourful employee to spend the rest of his life with his widowed mother, who still lived in the village.

He decided to live the rest of his life contemplatively, far away from the big cities, but could never renounce his profession as a doctor. He treated the destitute population free of charge in his treatment rooms.

After the death of his mother he went to Tenerife, where he died on 10 June 1868 at the age of 66. The house where he spent the last years of his life was transformed into the **Casa Mueo Dr. Mena** Museum in order to preserve the memory of him.

In his will of 1864 he left 25,000 pesetas for the construction of a hospital. In 1901 the construction work began on the

Hospital San Conrado y San Gaspar, which was stopped in 1929 despite sufficient funds from the inheritance.
The island government completed the building, which never took on the function of a hospital and today houses the tourist information office.

31 Antigua

The area around **Antigua** was one of the oldest agricultural regions of the island, but was not settled until 1560, when the feudal lords had their seat in **Betancuria** and kept the farmers under control. In 1812, 1834 and 1835 Antigua was declared the capital of the island for its economic importance, but lost all its importance in 1860 when the then **Puerto de Cabras**, now the **Puerto del Rosario**, became the seat of government.

At the entrance to the village, coming from Tiscamanita, a stately, pastel-coloured manor house in colonial style testifies to Antigua's former importance and wealth.

One of the sights of the city is the church of **Nuestra Señora de la Antigua,** inaugurated in 1784.

One of Antigua's greatest attractions is the windmill, the **Molino de Antigua** with its attached cheese dairy museum, the **Museo de Queso Majorero.**

Behind the restored windmill, dating from the 17th century, is the Cheese Museum. The entrance is on the left side of the building.
From the inner courtyard on the left you enter the exhibition room 1, with information about the island as well as flora and fauna.

Exhibition room 3, located frontally in the courtyard, presents the history of Fuerteventura cheese, its typical characteristics and its economic importance for the island.
Exhibition room 2 is located to the left of the courtyard and focuses on the island's goats and cheese production.

From the roof terrace on the upper floor you can enjoy a fantastic view of the landscape.
In the inner courtyard, on the right-hand side, there is a souvenir shop selling typical island handicrafts and cheese.

Do not miss to make a detour into the **cactus garden of** the plant, which is a bit hidden behind the payment house on the left side.

Opening hours: Tuesday- Friday: 9.30- 17.30 o'clock, admission price: 2,00 €.

32 Valles de Ortega

4 km south of Antigua, on the FV-20, is the small village of **Valles de Ortega**, which shares the **Ermita de San Roque** with the neighbouring municipality of **Casillas de Morales.** The church was founded by farmers in 1732 after a long plague epidemic.

The ruins in **Casillas de Morales**, which are to be seen on the field directly beside the road, offer beautiful photo motives.

33 Tiscamanita

An old windmill, which is the most prominent point of the town, prompted the island government to build a **Centro de Interpretacion de Molinos, an interpretation centre for windmills.**

At the entrance you will receive a German brochure with explanations on grinding tools such as mortars, hand mills, millstones, the grinding process, the production of gofio and the different types of windmills.

The restored miller's house and the windmill can be visited.

Opening hours: Tuesday- Saturday: 10.00- 17.30 o'clock, admission: 2,00 €.

If you follow the road sign "Centro de Interpretacion Los Molinos" in the Calle Los Molinos, turn left at the next possibility and at the end of the village you will find the **Ermita de San Marco,** which lies behind a high whitewashed wall. According to the inscription above the portal, it dates from 1699, but is permanently closed.

33.1 *Windmills - Molina or Molino?*

Windmill in Spanish means Molino, but not all windmills are the same.

At the beginning of the mill's history there was the single-storey, rectangular Tahona, a draught mill whose millstones were set in motion by people, donkeys or camels.

In the 17th and 18th centuries a two-storey windmill, a **Molino**, was imported from Spain. It is round, has a conical structure and a pointed roof made of wood or sheet metal. The mechanism, which is driven by 4- 6 wings, is located in the upper part on a rotating wooden double ring. The roof with the wings is rotated in the wind direction via an axis.

Since the millstones are located in the upper part of the Molino, the grain sacks were carried up an external staircase. The ground material then fell down wooden shafts and was filled into sacks.

In the 19th century, the introduction of the **Molina** simplified the workflow. The grinding mechanism was now only located in a single-storey building with a windmill turning on its flat roof. The wind power was transferred to a connecting rod which set the millstones in motion in the mill room.

33.2 The windmill route

On Fuerteventura there are still **23 Molinos** and **15 Molinas,** which can be discovered from north to south: Corralejo, El Roque, Villaverde, Tefía, Llanos de la Concepcíon, Antigua, Valles de Ortega, Tiscamanita and Puerto de Lajas.

Explore the historic mills, most of which have been restored, and those that are also decaying away from the main road.

In Pajara there is an old waterwheel in front of the church, so seen a Tahona, which is driven by a donkey when tourists are present.

34 Las Playitas

Next to the small picturesque **fishing village Las Playitas** there is the huge holiday resort **Playitas Grand Resort** with golf and tennis courts as well as a diving, surfing and sailing school.

At the hotel complex a path leads directly to the dark sandy beach **Las Playitas**.

Worth seeing: In the village, the FV-511 leads to the signposted **lighthouse Faro Punta de Entallada,** which is reached after 6 km. After a short drive, one discovers already from a distance the tower complex that stands on a 185 m high volcanic mountain.

The lighthouse was first switched on on 03 December 1954 and was one of the last large lighthouses to be built on the Canary Islands.
In front of the lighthouse a path leads to the viewpoint from where you can enjoy a wonderful view over the sea.
The way back again offers beautiful views of the landscape.

35 Gran Tarajal

A long avenue of palm trees leads to **Gran Tarajal** directly into the centre of the village, where most of the locals live.
The church of San Diego de Alcalá, built in 1900, is located at the entrance to the village. It is closed outside the fair. Directly opposite, under shady trees, lies a seahorse fountain.

In front of the deep, long, brown sandy beach **Playa de Gran Tarajal**, which is also suitable for children for bathing, runs the promenade with many cafés and restaurants.
At the end of the village is the marina, the front part of which is decorated with a whale skeleton.

36 Tarajalejo
The originally small fishing village **Tarajalejo** was extended with many apartments, a hotel complex and a long promenade that runs parallel to the black beach, the **Playa de La Tarajalejo.**

A wide wooden bridge leads over a Barranco, which in case of heavy rainfall leads the rainwater into the sea and divides the village into 2 parts.

Mareseum: In order to give the promenade a new splendour, five impressive sculptures were erected in November 2017 that "represent and convey the sea and everything it represents". The ensemble of the open-air museum is explained on display boards.

37 La Lajita
Passing dark brown volcanic mountains and small bays with black lava stone beaches, the FV-2 leads to **La Lajita**, a

small nest of new buildings. The **Ermita de la Inmaculada**, which is only open during fairs, is located on the dark stone beach **Playa de La Lajita**.

The real highlight of the place is the **Oasis Park**.

It is the second largest animal park in the Canary Islands after Loro Park in Tenerife.

More than 3,000 animals from 230 species as well as the largest cactus garden in Europe can be visited on an area of 800,000 square metres.

In the beautifully designed complex you will find a wide variety of monkeys, flamingos, meerkats, crocodiles, otters, lynxes, giraffes, hippos, cheetahs, coatis, deer, camels, elephants, llamas, zebras, gazelles, emus and pelicans.

There are also 4 live shows several times a day: Parrot Show, Sea Lion Show, Reptile Show and the Bird of Prey Show.

Important to know: The journey can be made individually by rental car, or free of charge with the organized buses of the Oasis Park from all holiday resorts of the island. You can find out the exact transfer times at the reception of the hotel.

Due to the size of the park, you should plan a whole day for the Oasis Park in order to be able to enjoy all the attractions. If one also wants to see all the live shows that each last approximately 45 minutes, one should build up the visit of the complex around the shows. Since the ways are very long, one usually does not manage to see all shows.

Parrot show: 9.45/ 10.45/ 11.45/ 12.45
Sea lion show: 11.15/ 15.45
Reptile Show: 12.00/ 14.00
Bird of prey show: 13.15/ 15.00

For the attractions with costs you have to buy the tickets at the ticket office in order to participate:

Camel safari, on the back of a camel caravan, Sea Lion Experience, swimming with sea lions, or the Lemur Experience, to experience monkeys up close.

By the way: The facility is very child-friendly. Several playgrounds are available so that the little ones can let off steam.

Hand wagons are available for a fee to make the long distances easier for the children. At the main attractions you can also buy food bags for the animals for a fee.

Electric scooters with 1 or 2 seats, as well as hand carts and children's bicycles are available for a fee.

Farmers' and craftsmen's market: Every Sunday from 9.00 a.m. to 1.00 p.m. there is a market worth seeing, where exclusively handmade products and local food are offered.

38 La Pared

From **Costa Calma,** towards **La Pared**, there is the narrowest part of the island called **Istmo de la Pared,** translated the isthmus of the wall. Legend has it that a wall separated the greater part of Fuerteventura called **Maxorata** from the **Jandía** peninsula. This stone wall is said to have separated the two existing kingdoms, but this has never been proven archaeologically.

It is impressive how the landscape changes on the FV-605 from **Costa Calma** towards La Pared. Shortly before La Pared, the barren, sandy desert landscape turns into light brown rock.

In the village, towards the Bahia Pared restaurant, there are two beaches next to each other, the **Playas de La Pared**, where there are strong undercurrents.

To reach the third beach, **Playa del Viejo Rey**, which is mainly frequented by surfers, go straight through the town. From the hill you have a beautiful view of the coast. On the right side you can see the **rock gate**.

The Queseria La Pastora, opposite the entrance to the village, is worth a visit.

Cheese made from sheep's and goat's milk is offered, there is the possibility to try all sorts.

39 Mirador Astronomico de Sicasumbre

The **viewpoint Mirador Astronomico de Sicasumbre** is located on the FV-605 between **La Pared** and **Pájara**. It was originally planned to observe the night sky, but also offers beautiful views during the day. The car can be parked on the side stripes. The ascent takes about 20 minutes.

40 Costa Calma

The popular holiday resort **Costa Calma** was founded in 1977 with the construction of the first hotel, the Solyventura, and is now one of the largest holiday resorts in the south of the island.

Until 2014, the FV-2 directed all traffic through the small wood of the village, which was planted with palm trees and pines.
In the meantime, the extended new motorway has made a large curve through the dunes of the nature reserve around the village, so that a peaceful silence has returned to the former through road.

The lively town offers numerous shopping and entertainment opportunities in addition to the shopping centres, the Centros Comerciales.

An **Africa market** takes place every Wednesday and Sunday from 9.00 - 14.00 near the lower roundabout of the town, towards the motorway.

The relatively narrow beach **Playa Costa Calma**, where sunbeds and parasols can be rented for a fee, is stocked with thick pebbles at low tide.

41 Playas de Sotavento

Directly adjacent to the **Costa Calma**, the most beautiful and longest sandy beaches of Fuerteventura, the **Playas de Sotavento**, begin, stretching to the south to **Morro Jable.**

The 16 km long coastal and beach section of Playa de Sotavento starts at Hotel Melía Gorriones with **Playa Barca**. In this area you will find the René Egli Wind- and Kitesurf Eldorado. Especially in the shallow, but tidal lagoon, beginners as well as professionals get their money's worth. Despite a section with sunbeds and umbrellas in front of the center, it is not suitable for swimming.
Immediately after **Playa Barca** follows the beach section **Risco de Paso**, which can also be reached by car.

42 Playas de Jandía

After the **Risco de Paso,** take the FV-2 motorway to **Morro Jable** and exit at 77 **Mal Nombre**. Following the signs, you

come to an abandoned hotel at the lower roundabout, behind which a road leads to the beach.
To the beaches of the **Playa de Butihondo** and the **Playa de Esquinzo,** one can walk from here at low tide on the beach, otherwise one follows the FV- 602, or takes the exit 79 from the motorway.

To the signposted **Playa Butihondo**, after the Fuerteventura Princess Hotel and before the Magic Life, a parking lot follows on the left side, from which a runway leads down to the beach.
From here, at low tide, you can reach the main beaches of **Jandía** on foot, the first of which is **El Saladar, located in** front of the Iberostar complex. Alternatively, the end of the highway FV-2, direction **Morro Jable**, leads directly to this beach.
The 100-hectare nature reserve is one of the special ecosystems of Fuerteventura, where salt marshes and plants have formed that grow in salt water despite the tides of the Atlantic.
The direct access to the beach is via paths.
Beach runners reach the lighthouse in a southerly direction, otherwise one gets into the rental car again and heads for the centre of Jandía city.

Towards **Morro Jable**, in front of the RIU Palace - Hotel Jandía, there is the **Playa de Matrorral**, probably the most beautiful part of the beach. Even if at the whole Playa **de Jandía,** the yellow or red flag already signals a bathing prohibition, one can swim here without reservations in the Atlantic. Crystal clear water, children can easily play on the beach and jump into the sea under supervision. Simply a fantastic beach location.

43 Risco del Paso
After the **Costa Calma** follow the huge snow-white dunes at the **Playa de Sotavento**, which were named after the 253 m high mountain range El Paso, also **Risco del Paso.**
The beautiful sandy beaches almost merge into **Playa de Butihondo** and **Playa de Esquinzo.**

Important for beach runners: Please note the tides, as **Playa de Sotavento** in particular is no longer passable at high tide.

44 Jandía

Jandía is the largest holiday resort in the south of the island. Due to the almost endless, dreamlike snow-white sandy beaches, the first hotel complexes were already built in the 1960s. Even in the 1970s, the transfer bus from the airport to the popular German holiday home took almost 4 hours. The transfer time has now been reduced to 1.5 hours due to better roads and motorway sections.

From the **El Saladar nature reserve**, with its unique plants that can grow in the salt water of the Atlantic despite the high and low tides, the breathtaking snow-white beach leads directly from the **Faro de Morro Jable** lighthouse to **Playa del Matorral**.

The centre of the retort city offers, besides a long beach promenade with modern sculptures running parallel to the sea, a long mile with bars and shopping facilities to find suitable souvenirs for your home.

The weekly **Africa Market** takes place on Mondays and Thursdays, next to the main road at the end of the village, towards **Morro Jable.**

45 Morro Jable

From **Playa de Matorral,** the promenade leads to the former, tiny fishing village of **Morro Jable**, where many restaurants are now lined up directly next to each other.

The end of the village is marked by a high rocky promontory on which houses and apartments are located, primarily for the locals who work in the hotels.

Then follows the **Puerto de Morro Jable**, the great **port of** Morro Jable, from where the ferries cross to Gran Canaria and Tenerife.

In the harbour of Morro Jable there is a **breeding station** for **sea turtles**, in order to settle these again at the coasts of the island.

The Canary Islands are part of the Caretta caretta, the hawksbill turtle, the leatherback turtle, the green turtle and the hawksbill turtle.

During the summer months, **hawksbill turtles** go to the coasts of Fuerteventura for food, especially to the quiet **Playas de Sotavento**.
Due to the increased tourism, however, the turtles do not find the necessary rest to lay their eggs, so that the population has shrunk enormously.
For the project, turtle eggs will be brought from the Cape Verde Islands to Las Palmas in Gran Canaria to be pre-bred at the Marine Science Institute ICCM and then buried for hatching on the beach of **Cofete**. After successful hatching, the babies are collected, raised in the breeding station and finally released into the sea again in Cofete.
Since turtles only reach sexual maturity after 15 years and return to the place where they were born to lay their eggs, it is hoped that in the foreseeable future the loggerhead turtle will resettle permanently on the coasts of the island.

Opening hours: Mon-Fri 10.00-13.00, free admission.
By the way: For the new edition in 2019, the lift station was closed for an indefinite period due to reconstruction measures. Please inform yourself on site about the current status.

46 Cofete
Just before the port of **Morro Jable** there is a signposted road from the FV-2 to **Cofete** and **Punta de Jandía** with the **lighthouse Faro de Jandía**.

After 1.6 km, on the right-hand side of the road, you come to the **cemetery**, the **Cementerio,** which is open with a little luck.

After the cemetery the asphalting of the road ends abruptly so that a rough shaken adventure can begin.
The long runway leads to the south point of Fuerteventura to the **Faro de Jandía**, the **turn-off to Cofete** is indicated with a large sign.
Arrived at the **pass**, the **Punto de Vista sobre Puerto de Montaña,** where one is almost blown away, one enjoys a fantastic view of **Cofete** and the **Barlovento** coast with the **Playa de Barlovento**.
The serpentines lead to the beach. At the wayside cacti grow in the lower area due to a different climatic zone.

Already from a distance one discovers a small settlement in which there is a small restaurant.

The piste leads automatically to the beach, as long as one does not drive to the restaurant. On the right you can see a building, the **Villa Winter,** which is signposted.
On the beach is the small orphaned **cemetery of Cofetes**.
The endless beach **Playa de Barlovento** invites to long beach walks. **Undercurrents provide deadly bathing accidents every year.** Lifeguards are not available!

On the way back you should visit **Villa Winter.**
The entrance is at the back of the property. The entrance is free, donations for the preservation of the property are gladly accepted.

In the exhibition rooms, a notice posted by the owner provides the following information: "Dear visitor, I am delighted that you have made the journey to Villa Winter. Surely you have heard many stories about this house. This building, with its inhabitants and history, was left to its own devices and to decay a long time ago.

I am Pedro Fumero and 3 years ago I left my job, my family and my work behind when I found my uncle and my aunt here in the villa. Two old, mentally handicapped people left to their own devices. It broke my heart and I came back to this house where I had spent a lot of time as a child. Since that day I have not stopped maintaining the house and uncovering the history of the legendary house of the Winter family. I am very grateful for your support in maintaining the house. Pedro Fumero."

The lonely situated **Villa Winter** with its high round tower is dilapidated and presented the highlight of the southern tip of Fuerteventura. The walls are full of legendary rumours: Hitler is said to have commissioned Gustav Winter, the owner of the villa, to set up a submarine base in the south of the island to control the shipping routes across the Mediterranean to America. Göring is said to have commissioned him to build factories...
Rumors or truth? - Biography and history meet:

Gustav Winter was born in 1893 in Neustadt in the Black Forest. During the First World War he spent time abroad, visiting Argentina and England, among other places.

- In 1915 Gustav Winter came to Spain via England.
- In 1921 he finished his technical studies in Madrid, which he had begun in Germany, and began to work on various projects.
- In 1924, at the age of 28, engineer Winter built the power station Cicer on Las Palmas in Gran Canaria, which was opened on 21.10.1928.
- In 1933, the year Hitler took office, Winter went to the Jandía peninsula.
- In 1937 Winter planned to build a cement factory and a fish factory in Jandía, but these were never built.
- In July 1937, Winter signed a lease with the heir of the Conde de Santa Coloma of Lanzarote for the entire Jandía peninsula. In the same year he travelled to Berlin to receive the necessary financial support for a project, whereupon he returned to Fuerteventura in the summer of 1938 with a small expedition of experts aboard a ship to explore the area, take photos and produce maps.
- During this time, Gustav Winter was already active as an agent of the German Defense in Spain. In a meeting between Winter and Defense III-Canarias it was agreed that Winter should carry out economically important projects for the German Reich in Jandia and receive German aid workers in return.
- From 1939 to 1944 he managed a shipyard of the German Navy near Bordeaux in France.
- From 1939, the entire Jandía peninsula was closed, and the few locals were resettled.
- At a meeting in October 1940 between Hitler and General Franco, Hitler announced that he wanted to establish a base on one of the Canary Islands, which General Franco initially rejected because of Spain's sovereign stance.
- However, between March and July 1941, 6 German submarine stations existed in the port of Las Palmas on Gran Canaria.
- In April 1941, the company "Dehesa de Jandia S.A.", whose manager was Gustav Winter, bought the Jandía peninsula.

- He met his wife in Madrid in 1945, a year later he started building the Villa Winter and the road to Cofete, which was built by political prisoners.
- It was not until 1947 that the Allies allowed the couple to return to the Canary Islands. Gustav Winter planted a tomato plantation, had wells built and tried to reforest the mountains of Jandia.
- According to local people, there were explosions on the peninsula for days in 1950.
- In 1962, the "Dehesa de Jandia S.A." approx. 2,300 ha land between Morro Jable and Cofete to Gustav Winter, as compensation for the development of the peninsula. When tourism began in 1966 with the construction of the first hotels in Jandía, the Winter family had taken care of themselves, as they received the equivalent of € 78.00 per square metre for the wasteland.
- In 1971 Winter died at the age of 78 in Las Palmas on Gran Canaria.

Public transport - Morro Jable - Cofete - Punta de Jandía

Line 111 departs daily at 10.00 and 14.00 from the central bus station, the **Estacíon de Guaguas** in **Morro Jable**, **Cofete** and **Punta de Jandía** with the lighthouse.

The bus is a Mercedes off-road vehicle, which covers the bumpy routes relatively comfortably within shortest time.

Already after 40 minutes one reaches the **Playa de Barlovento** in **Cofete**.

When leaving the bus, the return journey takes place at 12.45 or 16.45 hrs. After another 30 minutes the bus arrives at **Punta de Jandía.**

After a 45- minute break the journey continues at 12.00 or 16.00 o'clock.

From the lighthouse we go again to **Cofete**, with a 15 minute break. The journey to **Morro Jable** continues at 12.45 and 16.45 respectively.

Conclusion: The public bus is the only alternative to the rental car to reach the southern tip of Fuerteventura.

At the beginning of the journey it is not obvious that only the one-way journey costs 8,70 €. On arrival at Cofete, the driver points out the bus pick-up times, but does not mention that the journey continues immediately to the lighthouse. If one stays sitting in the bus, the continuation of the journey definitely ends with the exit at the lighthouse with a 45-minute break. Afterwards the fare of 8,70 € is due again to start the return journey to Morro Jable, which again runs via Cofete with a 15 minute stop.

In total you are on the road for 3.5 hours. Please note that the exhibition rooms of the lighthouse are closed in the meantime and that there are no toilets available for the direct exit of the bus.

47 Puerto de la Cruz
From **Morro Jable** there is a 20 km long dirt road to **Punta de Jandía**, with the **lighthouse Faro de Jandía**. Only the last short piece was asphalted.

At the big windmill is the small village **Puerto de La Cruz**, which consists of some fishing houses, 2 restaurants and a fixed caravan settlement.

The road leads to Punta de Jandía with its automatic lighthouse. In the former house of the lighthouse keeper there was a permanent exhibition about the flora and fauna of the island.

Please note that there are no sanitary facilities left.

48 Museum network on Fuerteventura
The **Red de Museos de Fuerteventura**, **Fuerteventura's museum network,** includes the following facilities - from north to south:

- **Museo de la Pesca Tradicional, in El Cotillo**
- **Cueva del Llano, in Villaverde,** currently closed
- **Museo del Grano La Cilla, in La Oliva**
- **Casa Alta de Tindaya, in Tindaya**
- **Ecomuseo La Alcogida, in Tefía.**
- **Casas de Felipito, in Altos de Guisguey**
- **Casa Museo Unamuno, in Puerto del Rosario**
- **La Ampuyenta, in Ampuyenta**

- **Mirador de Morro Velosa, in Morro Velosa**
- **Museo Arqueológico de Betancuria, in Betancuria,** in renovation since June 2017
- **Museo del Queso Majorero, in Antigua**
- **Museo de la Sal, in Las Salinas**
- **Los Molinos, in Tiscamanita.**
- **Poblado de La Antalayita, in Pozo Negro**
- **Faro de la Entallada, in Las Playitas**
- **Faro Punta de Jandía, in Puerto de la Cruz**

Tip: To make sure that the museums are open during your visit, it is advisable to have someone from the hotel reception in Spanish call the central office of Mon-Fri between 08.00 and 15.00 hours on the number: 928 85 89 98 to confirm the opening hours.

49 The history of goat cheese

Cheese as a foodstuff: Due to a lack of historical records, it is no longer possible to determine when the production and consumption of goat cheese began in Fuerteventura.

Majorero cheese is inseparable from the history of the island and its inhabitants, the majos. Only the production of cheese made it possible to process, store and store surplus milk.

Since Fuerteventura was occupied by North African Berbers for over 1000 years, the first settlers, whose main activity was livestock breeding, used the knowledge and experience of the Berbers to make cheese.

Trade and traditional production: In the 15th century, when Europeans sought trade routes to the New World across the Atlantic Ocean, the Canary Islands played a major role due to their favourable geographical location. European traders came together on the islands to conduct regional, retail and foreign trade.

In contrast to the other Canary Islands, Fuerteventura, as Isla de Señorio, had the right to levy levies of one fifth and impose restrictions. On the island a local, regional and interinsular trade took place.

The local trade was most strongly represented and was handled by merchants with shops, merchants who traveled across the island and cheese sellers.

Dr. Rene Vernau wrote in detail about this in 1884-1888, describing the livestock, the farm work, the shepherds and the traditional cheese production: "... The production is very simple. After milking, rennet is immediately added to the milk so that it coagulates and it is filled into simple round forms made of wood shavings and palm wood, which are placed on a board. Pressure is applied by hand to the curdled milk until the whey has escaped and the cheese has a firmer consistency. Now the cheese must be rubbed with salt and dried. When it's dried, it's so hard you can only share it with a stone or a hammer. The cheese is often additionally rubbed with clay on the outside, which gives it a somewhat appetising appearance. This procedure ensures that the cheese does not "harden".

Cheese making: The tradition of handmade goat cheese, Majorero cheese, is deeply rooted in Fuerteventura. Almost everyone who keeps goats makes cheese for their own use and sells the surplus.

The following operations are necessary for production: milking the goats, collecting the milk, adding ferments and rennet, cutting the curd, draining, moulding, salting, maturing and coating the cheese.

Traditional production methods have been passed down from generation to generation, but are now being replaced by modern techniques to ensure better hygiene conditions and produce larger quantities.

The secret of goat cheese: the Majorera goat is a native breed from Fuerteventura, which has adapted perfectly to the environment. Since the beginning of goat breeding, the farmers have carefully selected the animals, resulting in an extremely robust and resistant breed. The udders of the goats are very large, in animals with high milk production comparatively exaggeratedly large. The quality of goat's milk is very good, thick, aromatic and fatty, which is one of the most important secrets of goat's cheese.

Characteristics of the cheese: The production of Canary Islands goat's cheese is part of the cultural heritage of the Autonomous Community of Islands.

First and foremost, the cheese is made from raw goat's milk, which is of high quality and gives the product a special taste, smell and appearance.

Each island produces its own cheeses, for example the cheese of Fuerteventura Queso Majorero, La Palma Queso Palmero and Gran Canaria Queso de Flor de Guía.

Young goat cheese has a light rind that turns yellowish as it matures. Brushing with paprika, olive oil or gofio gives the cheese a different appearance.

Designation of Origin: The genuine Queso Majorero has a control label that guarantees the origin and quality of the raw materials, as well as the production and ageing process.

The designation of origin is based on regulatory criteria which must be met by all cheeses bearing it.

The islanders in harmony with the livestock: Before the arrival of the Europeans, the islanders called Fuerteventura Mahoh, translated, my country.

Historically it is not known when they arrived, but it is certain that they brought goats and shepherd dogs with them.

The goats were the most important livelihood of the people: they were used for milk and meat production. Clothes and shoes were made from the hides, the tendons served as sewing threads, the bones as needles; they constructed flights from leather and sticks hardened over fire.

They used leather and melted tallow as medicines and used butter, which they extracted from goat's milk, to heal wounds.

The shepherd dogs, which call themselves Majorero Canario, can be recognized by their grey-brown tabby skins.

Currently: The shepherds on Fuerteventura still milk small herds manually, from 60- 100 goats milking rooms with parallel systems are used to increase production capacity and hygiene conditions.

49.1 Belido Queseria

The Belido dairy is located in Tiscamanita, in the direction of Antigua, where the Mill Interpretation Centre is also located.

After entering the town, turn right into Calle San Marcos, keep left at the fork and follow the road to the end.

At the entrance there is a clamp timbre, which you have to press, shortly afterwards the shop is opened.

You can choose between medium and mature goat cheese with paprika, gofio or olive oil and cream cheese. There is also goat yoghurt and delicious gofioke biscuits with a dark and light chocolate coating, the Albajores de Gofio.

Opening hours: Mondays to Fridays 8.00 - 14.00 and 16.00 - 20.00, Saturdays and public holidays 8.00 - 14.00, Sundays closed.

49.2 Benigno Queseria
On the way to Ajui, on the FV-621, at KM-5, there is the Benigno cheese dairy.
In addition to the classic cheeses, homemade almogrote, a spicy spread paste made from goat cheese, oil and paprika, is offered.

49.3 Queseria Cañada de Agando
The cheese dairy is located on the FV-2 near Tuineje. One can recognize them by the fact that there is a huge area with goats right beside the main road.

Unfortunately it is only possible to buy whole cheese loaves.

49.4 Queseria La Pastora
The dairy is located on the FV-605, opposite the entrance to La Pared.
Cheese made from sheep's and/or goat's milk is offered, there is the possibility to try all sorts.

49.5 Queseria Maxorata
The cheese dairy is situated on the FV-20 Gran Tarajal towards Tuineje. After the 2nd roundabout there is a car wash on the right hand side, Autolavado, immediately after that you see the cheese dairy Maxorata, whose entrance sign reminds of the price board of a petrol station.

Opening hours: Monday to Sunday 9.00- 16.00, Saturday 8.00- 13.00, closed on public holidays.

49.6 Casa del Queso- Cabrera Pérez
The dairy is located on the FV-2, direction FV- 50, km 7 in 35638 Antigua.
In the building complex, all the steps involved in the production of goat's cheese, from rearing goats to feeding, milking and the production of the final products, are described in detail.

The cheese produced can be tasted and bought in the sales room. Especially for children the feeding of the goats is worth seeing. Opening hours: Daily from 10.00 - 17.00 o'clock. Admission is free.

50 Aloe vera

For the travel guide, two of the almost countless Aloe Vera farms were visited to give you an impression of the range of products on offer.

The **Bio- Aloe Vera Farm Verde Aurora** is located at the FV-2 in **Tecinosquey**, in **Malpais grande**, between **Gran Tarajal** and **Pozo Negro**. Letterings on the mountains indicate the farm.

In addition to aloe vera products, olives, oils, jams, moss sauces and cheese are offered.
Outside you can see the Aloe Vera plants, olive trees and a goat herd made of wood.

The **Aloe Vera Farm Finca Canarias** is located directly at the FV-2, at the height of **Tuineje**.
The dedicated employees explain everything about the topic **Aloe Vera**, in the sales room a variety of products are offered.

According to company information: "One of the great difficulties in using Aloe Vera is its purity, which is essential for the effectiveness of important biochemical substances. Many Aloe Vera cosmetics are so heavily enriched with chemicals that there is no cellular activity left. Unfortunately, many of these products do not have a sufficient amount of aloe vera, and sometimes they do not work. In Finca Canarias Aloe Vera we remove the flesh of the Aloe Vera. We press it cold, so all the properties are preserved and we can offer a 99.7% pure Aloe Vera product. ..."

51 Adventure Tours Fuerteventura

Discover all the highlights of Fuerteventura from north to south on 5 impressive adventure tours.

51.1 The North Tour

Dreamlike Caribbean beaches meet shifting dunes and culture:
The tour starts in **Corralejo** on the FV-1 direction Playas Grandes. You drive through the natural park, the Parque Natural de Corralejo, directly through the shifting dunes and past the fantastic beaches.
After Playa del Porís, the white dune landscape abruptly changes into brown volcanic mountains. Follow the road and after Casas de Jablito, take the FV 102 towards La Oliva.

In **La Oliva** the following sights can be visited: The church **Nuestra Señora de La Candeleria**, the **Casa de Los Coroneles**, the **Ermita de Puerto Rico**, the **grain museum- La Cilla**, the art centre **Centro de Arte Canario- Casa Mané** and the **Casa del Inglés**.

Follow the FV-10 in the direction of **El Cotillo**. Visit the **Castillo de El Tostón**, the defensive tower, take a look at the **lime kilns** in the harbour and make a detour to the long **Playa del Castillo**.

From El Cotillo the coastal road leads north to the **Museo de la Pesca Tradicional** - the **Fisheries Museum**.

Further dreamlike bathing bays, the **Playas de Los Charcos**, are not far from the lighthouse, in northern direction.

51.2 The discovery tour in the centre of Fuerteventura
The tour starts in **Tuineje,** which can be reached via FV-20. Here you visit the **church San Miguel Arcangel**, with the altarpieces to the historical battle at **Tamasite**.
From here the FV- 20 leads to **Tiscamanita** with the **Centro de Interpretacion de Molinos-** the **Tiscamanita Interpretation Centre for Windmills**.

On the way you will meet the windmill, the **Molino de Antigua** with its cheese museum, the **Museo de Queso Majorero in Antigua.**

From Antigua the FV- 20 leads to **La Ampuyenta** with sights that belong to the island history: the **hospital, Hospital San Conrado y San Gaspar**, the **Ermita de San Pedro de Alcantara**, the birth house of **Frailito Andres** and the house **Casa Museo Doctor Mena**.

Heading north, turn off the FV-30 onto the FV-207 towards **Tefía** to the **Ecomuseo La Alcogida** open-air museum. This tour ends with a visit to a traditional rural village.

51.3 The perfect panoramic trip in the south
On this impressive route you experience the transitions of a Sahara desert along the country road into gently rounded

and smoothly polished volcanic landscapes with incomparable vantage points.

Coming from the south, the tour starts from **Costa Calma**, direction **La Pared**.

On the way there is the possibility to make a short stop at the **Mirador Astronomico de Sicasumbre** or to continue the journey.

Passing the village of **Fayagua**, with covered growing areas, a sign indicates that tomatoes are for sale at harvest time.

The FV- 605 leads directly to **Pájara**, passing an artificial palm tree avenue on the side of the road.

Here the church **Nuestra Señora de la Regla** and the fountain **Noria** are in the centre.

At the signposted FV-30, direction Betancuria, the panoramic drive leads past a lime kiln.

The extremely winding serpentines lead to the viewpoint of **Betancuria**, the **Mirador del Risco de la Peña, with a** view of the valley of the unrealised dam in Vega **de Río de Palmas**.

The FV-30 continues to the old island capital Betancuria.

On the way to the **Mirador de Morro Velosa is** the viewpoint Mirador **de Guise y Ayose**.

This is where the panoramic tour ends.

51.4 The Coastal Tour

The tour starts in the south of Fuerteventura, in **Costa Calma**. From the FV- 2 you reach **La Pared** through the roundabout.

Visit the beaches in the village or try goat cheese in the cheese dairy opposite the street.

The FV- 605 leads you through the brown volcanic landscapes, past the highest mountain of the region, the

Montaña de Cardon with 691 m to the **viewpoint Mirador Astronomico de Sicasumbre**.

Enjoy the unique volcanic landscapes on the way to Pájara and turn before the village on the signposted FV-621 to Ajui.

The tour ends with a visit to this incomparable stretch of coast.

51.5 The South Tour to the top of Fuerteventura
Just before the port of Morro Jable there is a signposted road from the FV-2 to Cofete and **Punta de Jandía** with the **lighthouse Faro de Jandía**.

The long runway leads directly to the southern tip of Fuerteventura to the **Faro de Jandía**, the **turn-off to Cofete**, is marked with a big sign.

Arrived at the **pass**, the **Punto de Vista sobre Puerto de Montaña,** where one is almost blown away, one enjoys a fantastic view of **Cofete** and the Barlovento coast, with the **Playa de Barlovento**.

Visit the historic **Villa Winter** and stroll along the kilometre-long beach.

Returning to Cofete at the junction, follow the road to the right, direction El Puertito, to the lighthouse.